UNDERSEA MISSION

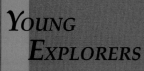

Library of Congress Cataloging-in-Publication Data
Jensen, Antony.
    Undersea mission.
    (Young explorers)
    Summary: Presents information on marine wildlife, underwater landscapes, diving history,
wreck diving, and diving dangers.
    1. Diving, Submarine--Juvenile literature. 2. Underwater exploration--Juvenile literature. 3.
Marine biology--Juvenile literature. [1. Diving, Submarine. 2. Underwater exploration. 3. Marine
biology] I. Bolt, Stephen. II. Title. III. Series: Young explorers (Milwaukee, Wis.)
GV840.S78J46   1989   796.2'3   88-42907
ISBN 1-55532-918-7

North American edition first published in 1989 by

Gareth Stevens Children's Books
7317 West Green Tree Road
Milwaukee, Wisconsin 53223, USA

US edition copyright © 1989. First published in the United Kingdom as
Underwater Dive with an original text copyright © 1989 Victoria House
Publishing Ltd.

Series editor: Valerie Weber
Research editor: Scott Enk
Cover design: Laurie Shock

1 2 3 4 5 6 7 8 9 94 93 92 91 90 89

YOUNG EXPLORERS

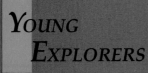

UNDERSEA MISSION

Written by Dr. Antony Jensen and Dr. Stephen Bolt
Illustrated by Paul Johnson

CONTENTS

Gareth Stevens Children's Books • Milwaukee

UNDERSEA PROFILE

The oceans of the Earth cover more than 70% of its surface. Over half of this is deep ocean, averaging 10,000 to 13,000 feet (3,000 to 4,000 m) in depth. The rest is shallow sea surrounding the world's seven land continents.

We have not yet explored much of the world's oceans. Diving expeditions are the best way for men and women to study this enormous area of our planet. Wildlife can be found in nearly every part of the ocean, so there is much to see and learn.

Arctic

Atlantic

Indian

Pacific

There are four oceans: the Pacific, the Atlantic, the Indian, and the Arctic. In each ocean, the temperature varies. For example, in the far north or south, the sea is cool, but around the Earth's equator, it is warm. Wildlife also varies in different ocean areas. Find out more about this on page 12.

The size of the oceans makes them difficult and expensive to study, so researchers have explored only small sections so far. They use underwater vehicles called submersibles to reach the deepest parts (see page 8).

Since the invention of scuba gear in the 1940s, divers have been able to explore the world's shallow seas.

Scuba gear includes a cylinder of compressed air that divers carry on their backs (see page 6). This gives scuba divers the freedom to move wherever they want.

Shallow seas are often the most interesting diving sites because they contain a rich variety of animals and plants, from warm-water coral reefs to cool-water seaweed forests. Find out more about different diving sites on page 12.

EXPLORING THE SEA

Diving expeditions go to sites for many reasons. Some of the most important reasons are shown in the boxes.

Diving biologists study marine animals and plants in their natural environment. With this information, we can learn how to conserve the world's oceans for everyone's benefit.

Marine archaeologists study shipwrecks and sunken cities to learn more about the past. By studying the contents of a wreck, for example, they can learn about the ship's cargo and about how the crew lived. To find out more about marine biology and marine archaeology, see pages 10 and 22.

Underwater photography experts dive in order to search for dramatic or unusual camera shots of wildlife and scenery.

Marine biologists and archaeologists also take photos on their dives. They can study the pictures and learn from them.

All divers must be trained by experts before going on a diving mission. They learn how to dive safely and how to use the correct equipment. They must also learn rescue and lifesaving skills.

EQUIPMENT LIST

If you were to go on a diving expedition, you would have to plan carefully in advance and check all your underwater equipment thoroughly to make sure it works properly. Some of the vital equipment you need for a dive is shown below.

A diving suit helps you to keep warm and protects you from sharp rocks and stinging creatures.

In very cold water, you need a waterproof dry suit so that you can put on warm woolen underwear beneath it.

In warmer water, you can wear a wet suit, which lets some water through to the skin. Your body heats this moisture, which helps to keep you warm.

Around your waist, you need a belt with heavy lead weights attached to help you swim toward the bottom. A pair of fins will help you swim more strongly.

A face mask allows you to see clearly under water. It also magnifies everything you see by a fourth, so animals and plants will look bigger than they really are.

When you dive, the water around you presses in on your body. The deeper you go, the higher the water pressure.

In order for your lungs to expand properly, the air you breathe in must push out with the same pressure as the water pushes in. You need a scuba tank for this.

Part of the scuba tank is a cylinder filled with compressed air. This means that the air molecules are squeezed together so that the air exerts a high pressure out.

A device called the demand valve regulates the air, supplying it at the same pressure as the water around you, no matter how deep.

When you dive from a boat, you need a line connecting you to a brightly colored buoy on the surface. That way, someone in the boat can follow your progress. Divers should never dive alone — in an emergency you may need help!

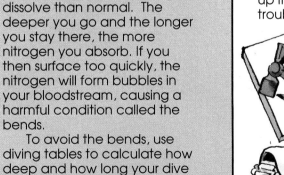

DIVING EXTRAS

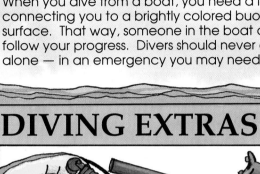

A knife cuts you free from any weeds or fishing nets.

A snorkel tube allows you to breathe on the surface.

An underwater flashlight helps you see at night or in murky water.

When you breathe in air, oxygen and nitrogen gases dissolve into your blood.

As you descend, the water pressure makes more nitrogen dissolve than normal. The deeper you go and the longer you stay there, the more nitrogen you absorb. If you then surface too quickly, the nitrogen will form bubbles in your bloodstream, causing a harmful condition called the bends.

To avoid the bends, use diving tables to calculate how deep and how long your dive should be. Also, wear an underwater watch to time yourself and a depth gauge to measure how deep you are.

A diver's life jacket keeps you buoyant on the surface and helps you float up if you are in trouble.

A depth gauge monitors how deep you are.

A hammer and chisel enables you to take rock samples. You can use a waterproof board and pencil for notes.

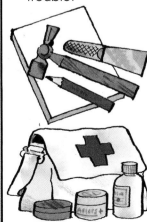

Don't forget the waterproof case and a flash gun for your underwater camera.

After a dive, you will need to shower in fresh water. Otherwise you could get salt-water skin sores. To treat these, add antiseptic creams and powders to your equipment list.

DEEP-SEA DIVING EQUIPMENT

Humans cannot dive in deep ocean water because the very high water pressure soon disturbs the body's nervous system. Instead, men and women use underwater vehicles called submersibles for jobs such as repairing pipelines and salvaging wrecks. They launch submersibles from ships that have expert back-up crews and equipment on board to track the submersible's movements.

Submersibles run on batteries and can stay under water for a few days at a time.

Inside the submersible, there must be a life-support system for the crew so that they can breathe and work comfortably. Only three or four people can fit into a piloted submersible.

On the sides of a submersible are observation windows, video cameras, spotlights, and mechanical arms. Divers move these by remote control to pick up samples or to use tools outside.

The suit shown above is a one-person submersible called JIM. It can take you down 2,000 feet (610 m).

Inside the suit there is a life-support system. Outside there are mechanical hands and joints that allow you to move.

The JIM suit is useful for getting into confined spaces where bigger submersibles cannot reach.

Scientists use ROVs and piloted submersibles to map the seabed and to study deep-sea wildlife, sometimes putting out bait to attract fish near the submersible to film them.

You can find out more about some of the deep-sea creatures seen from submersibles on page 18.

Unpiloted submersibles are sometimes called ROVs (Remotely Operated Vehicles). They usually have a cable linking them to the ship so that someone on board can steer and move any robot arms by remote control.

Video cameras transmit the underwater pictures to the surface. In deep, murky waters, ordinary cameras are useless, so ROVs are fitted with cameras that are sensitive to small amounts of light.

A diver who gets the bends by going too deep must be rushed into a decompression chamber, where air pressure is increased so that nitrogen bubbles dissolve back into the blood. Then the pressure is slowly brought back to normal.

When divers work a long time at great depths, their bodies become saturated, absorbing all the gases they can. So it is convenient for them to go up and down each day in a pressurized diving bell, spending their off-duty time in this pressurized chamber. When their job is done, they go into a decompression chamber to correct their internal pressure levels.

Diving bell

STUDYING THE SEA

Divers play a valuable part in increasing our knowledge of the oceans because they can study marine life close up, watching creatures in their natural habitat.

It can take years to plan an expedition to study deep-sea wildlife. The scientists must decide exactly what they want to study — for example, why a coral reef is being damaged, or how pollution is affecting an area of seabed.

You don't need to be a trained scientist to help with this work. For example, if biologists need to know which animals and plants live around a coastline, amateur divers can help by collecting samples and observing wildlife.

You could use waterproof boards and pencils for recording underwater sights, as well as plastic bags for taking samples to the surface for further study.

Photographs of underwater life are valuable to marine scientists who can study them in detail later.

To get a good shot, move as close as possible to your subject. Use a wide-angle lens to get as much of your subject in the picture as you can.

Once you've collected the wildlife samples, preserve and label them with their names and where they were found. Months of laboratory research often follow.

One example of underwater biology work is the study of coral reefs. Scientists have done some fascinating scientific experiments on them.

For example, by placing different kinds of coral together, divers have discovered that some types are aggressive, killing their neighbors by giving off destructive chemicals. This type of experiment takes a long time and can mean dives to the same site for months or even years.

The best way to study fish is in their natural environment, the ocean. But there are problems in trying to watch them under water — you might disturb the fish and frighten them away!

Fish can sense water pressure and flow changes caused by other creatures some distance away. They do this through a system of sensitive canals and openings along their body called the lateral line organs.

Lateral line

Diving geologists do important scientific work too. They explore areas chosen for tunneling or oil exploration, take samples of rocks or seabed, and bring them to the surface for study.

A DIVER'S SEA LIFE GUIDE

A wildlife community living in one particular area is called an ecosystem. Ocean ecosystems vary according to sea conditions such as depth and temperature.

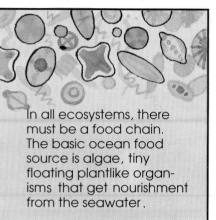

In all ecosystems, there must be a food chain. The basic ocean food source is algae, tiny floating plantlike organisms that get nourishment from the seawater.

Algae are eaten by fish, whales, and tiny animals and plants that are called plankton. But many creatures hunt other ocean animals for food.

At the end of the food chain, there are seabed creatures that eat dead material. When they digest this food, they break it down into nutrients which are recycled into the sea.

ROCKY SEABED

If you dive in a rocky seabed area, you are likely to see a wide variety of wildlife. A rock is a stable, solid surface for plants and animals to live on, while cracks and caves provide nooks and crannies for animals to set up home and hide from their enemies.

FLAT SEABED

Much of the seabed is flat and featureless. But that does not stop animals from living there. For example, many creatures live in the mud, burrowing down to hide from enemies. Sea cucumbers, worms, and crabs are common bottom-dwellers.

MIDOCEAN

Most ocean wildlife floats or swims near the sea surface in midocean, far from the shore or seabed. Many fish and jellyfish never venture near the shore or the sea bottom.

CORAL REEFS

With their wide variety of wildlife, coral reefs are ideal for divers interested in nature. The water is usually clear and good for photography. Sometimes you can even hear the sounds made by underwater creatures.

POLAR REGIONS

If you went diving under the polar ice, you would see many creatures living in the icy water. Millions of tiny, shrimplike creatures called amphipods live underneath the ice. Fish eat the amphipods, and creatures such as seals eat the fish as part of the polar food chain.

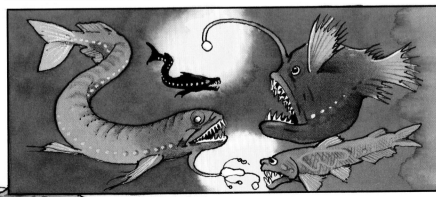

DEEP SEA

It is difficult to explore the deepest parts of the sea. Many areas are too deep for sunlight to reach, so the creatures that live there have developed features such as luminous spots to help them feed. You can find out more about this strange ecosystem on page 18.

THE SEA GARDEN

In shallow seas, the underwater landscape can look like a spectacular garden, made up of seaweeds and plantlike animals such as corals and anemones.

Corals are colonies of animals that live in warm, clear water. They are either hard or soft. They grow in many shapes — some look like fingers while others look like cabbage leaves or delicate fan-shaped skeletons.

Soft corals have an outside layer of living tissue around a central flexible stalk.

The tissue is home to many small anemone-like animals called polyps, which are connected to each other through their stomachs. They use tiny tentacles to catch food that they share.

Large corals are usually hard. They have a wall around them which is built when the polyps take calcium from the water and use it to surround themselves with what becomes a stony skeleton.

As the polyps grow and increase in number, the size of the coral increases. Eventually reefs are formed.

Brightly colored sponges and anemones are common coral reef animals. Many vividly marked fish are attracted to corals, often forming spectacular groups around them.

Some animals badly damage the reefs. For instance, the crown-of-thorns starfish feeds on coral polyps in warm water.

Crown-of-thorns

14

Behind a reef, there is often a shallow lagoon carpeted with sea grasses, the only true flowering plants in the ocean.

Sea grass meadows are nursery grounds for fish and feeding grounds for animals such as turtles. In some meadows, you might see a dugong, or sea cow.

Dugong

The kelp seaweed forests of the eastern Pacific are a spectacular sight, with seaweed towering up to 200 feet (61 m) high. The forests are famous for sea otters, which help the seaweed survive by eating the sea urchins that graze on the young kelp plants.

Sea otters

The otters dive to the seabed, pick up an urchin and a stone, and take them both up to the surface. They float on their backs and, using their chests as tables, they break open the urchin with the stone and eat its contents.

More beauty lies beneath the kelp blades, where sponges, anemones, and starfish reveal brilliant colors and unusual shapes to divers.

DANGEROUS ANIMALS

Among the many thousands of creatures in the sea, there are a few that can be harmful, sometimes even fatal, to humans.

There are two types of dangerous creatures divers need to look out for — the kind that bite and the kind that sting.

Sharks are the largest sea fish. Some species feed peacefully on plankton, but most sharks feed on other creatures and have powerful jaws filled with teeth.

Not all sharks are dangerous, but a few species will attack humans. Beware especially of the hammerhead shark, shown below, and the great white shark, which can grow up to 20 feet (6 m) long.

Shark attacks on divers are quite rare, but you increase the chances by spear fishing, since blood from a harpooned fish might attract hungry sharks. An attack is also more likely if you splash around on the water surface. The sharks might mistake you for wounded prey!

Some otherwise harmless fish can give you a painful bite if you disturb them. Watch out for moray eels in warm waters. They can grow up to 10 feet (3 m) long and have sharp teeth for inflicting nasty wounds.

Sea snakes are common in many areas. Sometimes their venom is more poisonous than that of any land snake. Luckily, they are usually not aggressive and will leave you alone unless they are frightened by sudden movements.

16

Some animals have poison-ous bites. For instance, you might find a blue-ringed octopus in the Indo-Pacific waters around Australia. The poison from its bite can swiftly cause you to suffocate.

One of the most dangerous sea creatures of all is the box jellyfish or sea wasp, which also lives in the Indo-Pacific. Its long tentacles inflict a sting that can cause death in minutes and at best leave a survivor's skin badly scarred. Anyone diving in an area with box jellyfish must always wear a protective suit.

European and Atlantic jellyfish are not as dangerous as the Indo-Pacific variety. One exception to this is the Portuguese man-of-war, which can give a terrible sting with its tentacles. It hangs beneath a gas-filled float that sticks up above the water.

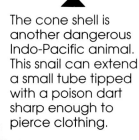

The cone shell is another dangerous Indo-Pacific animal. This snail can extend a small tube tipped with a poison dart sharp enough to pierce clothing.

The stonefish lives in warm waters. It looks just like a stone, so it could easily be touched by mistake. It delivers strong poison through its back fins.

There are several other fish with poisonous fins. One eye-catching example is the tropical lion fish, which has an unpleasant sting.

DEEP-SEA LIFE

Most sunlight cannot reach water deeper than about 2,000 feet (600 m), but there are some parts of the ocean more than 13,000 feet (4,000 m) deep! There are some unique animals adapted to a life in darkness at these depths. By diving in submersibles or examining specimens brought up in nets, scientists have recently found out more about some of them.

Deep-sea fish fall into four groups — nibblers, stalkers, ambushers, and hunters.

Nibblers are small fish that live between the deepest parts of the ocean and the lighter water above. They often have light spots on their bellies so that when seen from below, they do not show up against the background glow from the water surface. They sometimes try to confuse their enemies by flashing the lights on and off.

Many deep-sea fish have their own source of light, called bioluminescence, to attract prey or to confuse enemies. The light is caused by a chemical reaction on the surface of their skin.

Some nibblers look strange compared to ordinary fish. For example, the hatchetfish (shown enlarged above) has a flat, silvery body about 3/4 inch (2 cm) long and bulging eyes. Some hatchetfish have eyes pointing upward, so they can see prey above them.

Many fish hunt nibblers. Some of these are stalkers — fish which swim around stalking prey.

The dragonfish above is a stalker, growing up to 28 inches (71 cm). Below its chin, it has a tentacle called a barbel that ends in a light-producing bulge. Nibblers mistake the bulge for food and find themselves inside a mouth lined with fangs.

18

The fish in the hunter group are fast swimmers and chase after nibblers. Their teeth sometimes have hooks on them to make sure that their catch does not escape. The fangtooth fish is one example — it is only 6 inches (15 cm) long.

Some of the most unusual forms of deep-sea life were only recently discovered, when submersibles were used to explore life around hydrothermal vents. These are splits in the Earth's crust where hot gases and melted minerals and metals seep out into the sea.

Animals living in these vents include giant clams, blind crabs, and enormous red-tipped worms, 10 feet (3 m) long!

The deep-sea anglerfish shown below is an ambusher. It lurks on the seabed, waiting to ambush its unsuspecting prey.

The anglerfish has a series of rods for fishing sticking out from its head. Each one ends in a luminous tip. The fish waves its rods around to lure prey near. Then it grabs its victim with its sharp teeth.

SEA MAMMALS AND DIVERS

Of all the animals in the oceans, whales, dolphins, and porpoises are most closely related to humans. Like us, they are warm-blooded mammals, while fish are cold-blooded. These sea mammals are the most intelligent creatures in the sea and among the most interesting for divers to study.

There are two types of whale — baleen and toothed. Toothed whales, such as sperm whales, eat larger fish and squid. Instead of teeth, baleen whales have horny plates in their mouths that filter tiny floating animals called krill from the seawater. The blue whale, a baleen, is the largest animal in the world, growing up to 100 feet (30 m) long.

You can tell dolphins and porpoises apart by their shapes. Porpoises have blunt snouts and fat bodies; dolphins are bigger, with longer snouts.

Dolphin

Blue Whale

Even though we have seen whales beneath the sea, we've made our best observations near the surface of the water, where whales will sometimes let humans come near.

Despite this, diving is the best way to study whales at close range. One example of a useful discovery made at close range occurred on a diving expedition organized to observe sperm whales in the Indian Ocean. The divers found out a lot about the behavior of the whales and were the first to see a sperm whale born.

Porpoise

There are still some mysteries about sea mammals that divers could help solve in the future.

For example, whales can dive to great depths for long periods of time, but we do not yet know how their bodies can tolerate the high water pressure at deep levels.

Whales, dolphins, and porpoises make sounds such as clicks, barks, and whistles. When they are in groups, they use these sounds to talk to each other, but humans can't understand their language yet.

Sea mammals also use sound to detect things in the dark. They make a sound and then detect the returning vibrations that have bounced off objects in their path.

Whales are hunted for use in many commercial products. This has led to the near extinction of several species. Now conservationists are trying to limit the killing before it is too late.

Divers have helped in this battle by studying and filming whales. In this way, more people have become aware of their beauty and intelligence and the need to save these giants of the ocean.

HISTORY SEARCH

Diving archaeologists explore the remains of ships or sunken towns. As in land archaeology, an underwater excavation is called a dig.

It can take years to fully explore a dig, with much painstaking planning and hard work in the water and on the surface. Equipment must be looked after and reports written on the finds of each day.

They also make a survey of the dig site. Sometimes they place a large metal grid over the area and use it like a map for reference. Divers can also swing from it as they work. They use metal detectors and probes to explore the seabed.

It is not easy to find a wrecked ship. If it sank on rocks, the hull might have broken up and spread over a wide area. If it landed on a sandy or muddy seabed, it could be buried in sludge.

Archaeologists searching for a particular ship will look through many libraries and records, reading about where and how a ship sank and gathering clues on its possible location.

To pinpoint wrecks from the surface, archaeologists use magnetometers that detect the magnetism of metal objects. They also use sonars, bouncing sound waves off the seabed and measuring the time they take to return. They use this information to form a picture of the seabed.

To clear away mud and sand, divers use a dredge, a long pipe that acts like an underwater vacuum cleaner. As the air rises up the pipe, it sucks up mud and sand surrounding an object or area. They can alter the flow of air to excavate small objects or large areas.

Every object found on an archaeological dig is valuable as a possible historical clue. Each piece must be carefully cleaned, drawn, and photographed under water. It is important to record exactly where each object is found in a wreck site. This helps archaeologists decide how things were used and who might have owned them. For example, if an object comes from a ship's galley, it could have been used for cooking.

Divers gently lift finds to the surface for careful restoration. This can take some time. For example, wood has to be washed in fresh water for many days to remove the sea salt. Then it is soaked in a chemical to stop it from splitting and rotting. Conserving a very large wooden object, such as a ship's hull, can take up to 20 years.

Some objects last very well under water. One example is this barber-surgeon's chest from the *Mary Rose*, which sank off the coast of Britain in 1545. Inside were black pepper, ointment jars, and medical tools.

DIVING HISTORY

Although modern diving equipment was not developed until the 1940s, the history of diving goes back a long way.

The first known divers were people who gathered shellfish to eat and items they could sell, such as sponges and pearls. They could not stay under water for long so, to speed up their descent, they would tie rocks to themselves.

From ancient Greek times, divers have also salvaged treasure from sunken ships and hampered the enemy in sea battles.

We know that diving gear was used in ancient times, when divers used bamboo snorkels to swim below the surface.

From the 1300s on, many inventors started designing more complicated equipment. Even the great artist Leonardo da Vinci did some sketches of diving equipment in the 1500s. But most of these early ideas could never have worked in practice.

One of da Vinci's ideas

The *Turtle*

The wooden *Turtle* was one of the first working submersible designs. Built by a U.S. inventor named David Bushnell, it was used to attack a British ship off the U.S. coast in 1776.

The U.S. *Nautilus*, an 1801 submersible, could carry four people and had a hand-cranked propeller. It also had a sail that folded up like an umbrella when the ship was under water.

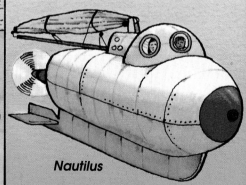

Nautilus

Once efficient air pumps were invented, diving suits became possible. They usually had heavy, glass-fronted helmets and were sometimes called hard hat suits.

In the 1800s there were many new designs. The Siebe suit, shown below, resulted. For safety, the whole Siebe suit was inflated with air. This made the divers very light, so they had to wear heavy boots and weights.

Hard hat divers needed an air line going up to the surface. The first person to design a self-contained suit was W.H. James. His idea was to carry an air supply inside a metal belt, as shown on the left. A similar suit was used by Charles Condert in New York's East River. He died while diving in 1832, when his air supply failed.

This 1808 suit design would never have worked. The diver wears a crown attached to a bellows and works it by nodding his head.

This strange and impossible device was designed in 1551. The diver is in a weighted, wooden frame, with his head inside a glass ball.

This diver has an early pressurized air tank. It was pioneered by two Frenchmen, Benoît Rouquayrol and Auguste Denayrouze.

MYTHS AND LEGENDS

For many centuries, the sea has been the subject of incredible tales and mysterious events. The black depths would make perfect homes for monsters and magical underwater kingdoms.

Modern divers have been able to explain many of the old stories, but there are still a few mysteries.

In many stories, half-fish, half-human mermaids come ashore as women, marry humans, and later disappear back to the sea. In Greek legends, beautiful maidens called sirens lured ships onto rocks.

These legends may have come originally from sightings of seals and dugongs (see page 15). In many mermaid stories, the moral is — strange sea creatures should be left alone!

The sailors of the past feared the attack of giant sea monsters. You can see pictures of them on many ancient sea maps. To sailors in a small boat, a spouting whale could have been mistaken for a monster.

One sea monster that does exist is the Atlantic giant squid. There are reports of these squids attacking boats. The body of the longest squid ever measured was over 20 feet (6 m) long, with tentacles that measured another 35 feet (10.5 m)!

26

The location of the *Titanic* was a twentieth-century mystery. This huge cruise liner was supposed to be unsinkable. But in 1912, it hit an iceberg in the Atlantic and quickly plunged to the sea bottom.

For years, divers searched for the remains, hoping to find the jewels and money rumored to be on board. In 1986 the wreck was explored, but few treasures remained.

Stories abound of wrecked Spanish ships, called galleons, loaded with gold. But any expedition would have to be carefully researched and well equipped to be successful in finding treasure.

One example of missing treasure is a hoard of 10 million gold coins thought to be lying near the coast of Peru. The coins were sent by Holy Roman Emperor Charles V to a group of Peruvian Catholics, but the ship sank before it reached its destination.

The legend of a lost underwater city called Atlantis has been around for over 2,000 years. The Greek writer Plato first mentioned it. He wrote of a terrible disaster when the seabed opened up and swallowed a whole continent.

Some people now think that the stories are based on a volcanic explosion in the Mediterranean. Others think it may have happened in the North Atlantic.

UNDERSEA FUTURE

Future scientific developments will probably lead to safer and easier diving in the world's oceans.

Researchers are now working on lighter, more comfortable diving suits and scuba tanks capable of carrying more air for breathing.

New materials could be developed for dry suits (see page 6). These could insulate divers against the cold more efficiently and make the suit less buoyant so divers would need fewer weights.

Small waterproof computers will probably become essential for divers to calculate the timing of their stay under water and the rate of their rise to the surface to avoid the bends (see page 7).

In the 1960s, Jacques Cousteau, the French diving pioneer, built an underwater house named Conshelf, to find out whether humans could live under water.

The air inside Conshelf was kept at the same pressure as the water outside. This caused problems for the inhabitants, and Conshelf was finally closed.

To avoid these difficulties, underwater houses could be built in shallow water where inside pressure could be kept at a level similar to the air pressure above the surface. The workers could stay under water for as long as they wanted.

Farming of the sea is called mariculture. Already scientists have built artificial reefs and seeded them with shellfish. In the future, mariculture is likely to become even more important. Experts may develop breeds of fish that are more resistant to diseases and parasites. Marine farm workers could live in underwater communities and till the sea.

FUTURE PARKS

As diving has become a more popular sport, it has threatened wildlife. A few years ago, divers would often take lobsters and crabs and use spear guns to kill fish.

More recently, underwater areas have been made into marine reserves, where divers take nothing except photographs. One of these reserves, the Coral Reef State Park in Florida, is dotted with beautiful underwater statues, such as the one shown on the left.

In addition to making sure that sea life is preserved, these areas give scientists a great opportunity to study underwater creatures in their natural habitat. These reserves will eventually provide a source of young animals to restock areas of the sea.

FOR MORE INFORMATION

Magazines

Here are some children's magazines that have articles about the seas and oceans and the animals and plants living there. If your library or bookstore does not have them, write to the publishers listed below for information about subscribing.

Dodo Dispatch
34th Street and Girard
Philadelphia, PA 19104

Elsa's Echo
3201 Tepusquet Canyon
Santa Maria, CA 93454

Owl
The Young Naturalist Foundation
59 Front Street East
Toronto, Ontario
Canada M5E 1B3

National Geographic World
National Geographic Society
17th and M Streets NW
Washington, DC 20036

3-2-1 Contact
Children's Television Workshop
One Lincoln Plaza
New York, NY 10023

Tracks
P.O. Box 30235
Lansing, MI 48909

Addresses

The organizations listed below have information about oceans and species living in or near them. When you write to them, tell them exactly what you want to know.

Greenpeace USA
1611 Connecticut Avenue NW
Washington, DC 20009

National Audubon Society
950 Third Avenue
New York, NY 10022

Save the Whales
P.O. Box 3650
Washington, DC 20007

Sierra Club
730 Polk Street
San Francisco, CA 94109

Books

You can read more about oceans, seas, and related subjects in the following books. If they cannot be found in your local library or bookstore, ask someone there to order them for you.

Children's Book of the Seas. Tyler and Watts
    (EMC Publishing)
Incredible Facts about the Ocean.
    Robinson (Dillon)
The Mysterious Undersea World. Cook
    (National Geographic Society)

Ocean Frontiers. Davies (Viking)
Oceans. Jennings (Marshall Cavendish)
Our Amazing Ocean. Adler (Troll)
The Sea is Calling Me. Hopkins
    (Harcourt Brace Jovanovich)
The World's Oceans. Sandok (Franklin Watts)

Glossary

Anemone
A meat-eating animal that looks like a flower. It has a short body with no skeleton and is shaped like a cylinder. It attaches at the bottom to a rock or the seabed. On top, around its mouth, is a crown of tentacles that can be retracted, or pulled in. It uses these tentacles to capture its prey. Over 1,000 species of anemones live in the ocean.

Bioluminescence
The discharge of light by certain animals. Most bioluminescent animals are saltwater fish but a few are insects. Usually bioluminescent fish give off a blue or blue-green light. This light is produced by the mixture of certain chemicals contained in the fish's body. The strength of the light depends on the amount of necessary chemicals present.

Buoyant
Capable of floating or of keeping things afloat.

Conservation
The protection, preservation, and management of the environment and the Earth's natural resources.

Galleon
A large sailing ship with three masts for sails. It usually has two or more decks, or floors. Galleons were used during the fifteenth and sixteenth centuries, especially for war or trading purposes.

Hydrothermal Vents
Cracks in the ocean floor from which hot water continually pours. First, cold seawater trickles down through these openings in the seabed. The water then picks up heat and dissolves minerals from the molten rocks welling up from the Earth's mantle, the layer between the Earth's crust and the core. Then the hot water gushes out, warming the surrounding water. This warmth permits an unusual variety of animals to grow. The dissolved minerals in the water sometimes form deposits around the hotter vents. These deposits look like chimneys.

Krill
Small, transparent, shrimplike animals that live in all the oceans. They are *bioluminescent* and eat both plants and animals. They, in turn, are an important source of vitamin A for many creatures in the sea. In the future, people might also use krill as a source of food for themselves or their animals.

Lateral Line
Organs on fish that detect slight vibrations made by other animals in the water. The lateral line is made up of small openings on a fish's body which lead to the actual sense organs. Usually the organs run down the sides of the body, but in some deep-sea fish, the organs are placed on stalks on their bodies or on their heads.

Polyp
A marine animal with a very simple structure. A polyp is basically shaped like a tube. One end, known as the foot, is closed and the other end, the mouth, is open. The mouth is usually surrounded by tentacles. When a live polyp is cut into large pieces, each portion can develop into a complete individual.

Seed
To plant or to sow. For example, scientists seed or place young lobsters and other shellfish into marine areas where they do not usually live. In this way, people can gather shellfish from a specific area and depend on it as a steady and convenient food source.

Sponge
An animal that resembles a plant. Sponges are one of the most primitive of the many-celled animals. They have branching stems and growths that look like leaves. There are 5,000 types of sponges, ranging in size from 1/2 inch (1 cm) to over 3 feet (1 m) across.

Index